OUR
BABY
Album

OUR BABY Album

SMITHMARK

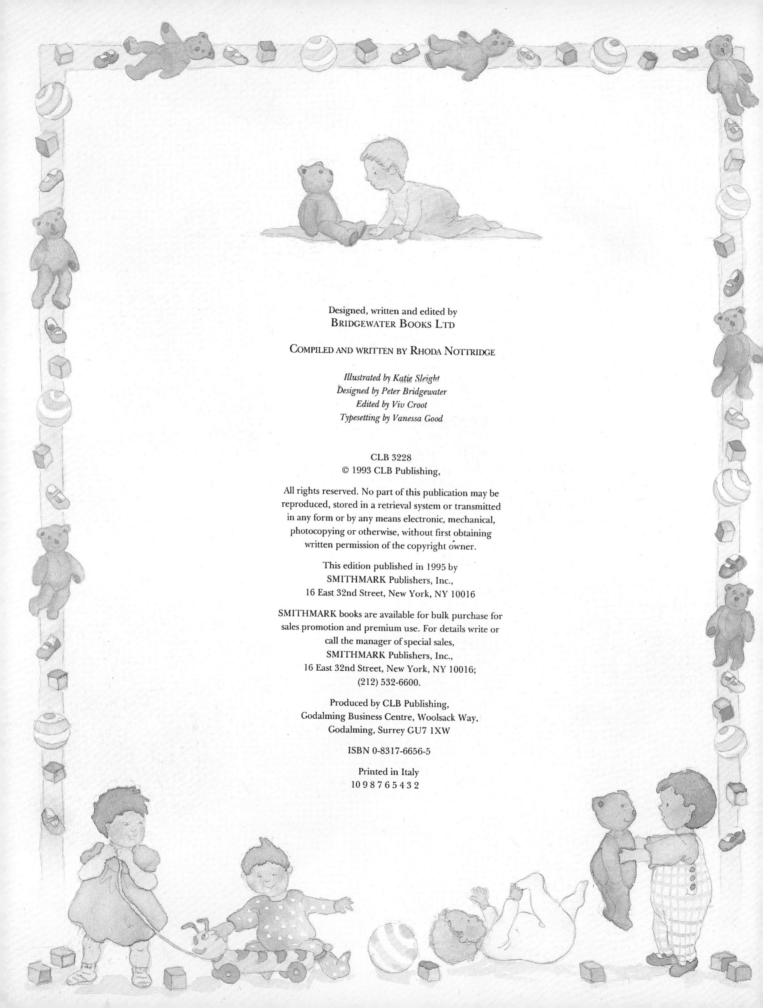

Designed, written and edited by
BRIDGEWATER BOOKS LTD

COMPILED AND WRITTEN BY RHODA NOTTRIDGE

Illustrated by Katie Sleight
Designed by Peter Bridgewater
Edited by Viv Croot
Typesetting by Vanessa Good

CLB 3228
© 1993 CLB Publishing,

This edition published in 1995 by
SMITHMARK Publishers, Inc.,
16 East 32nd Street, New York, NY 10016

SMITHMARK books are available for bulk purchase for
sales promotion and premium use. For details write or
call the manager of special sales,
SMITHMARK Publishers, Inc.,
16 East 32nd Street, New York, NY 10016;
(212) 532-6600.

Produced by CLB Publishing,
Godalming Business Centre, Woolsack Way,
Godalming, Surrey GU7 1XW

ISBN 0-8317-6656-5

Printed in Italy
10 9 8 7 6 5 4 3 2

CONTENTS

TO

WITH LOTS OF LOVE FROM

PHOTOGRAPH

T his album records the
early years of baby

WELCOME TO THE WORLD

This book is a permanent record and reminder of the greatest event in your life: the birth of your new baby. Fill these pages with photographs, mementoes and all those little details of baby's early years and your first times together. Treasure this book forever, so you can always remember these precious early days.

ARRIVAL

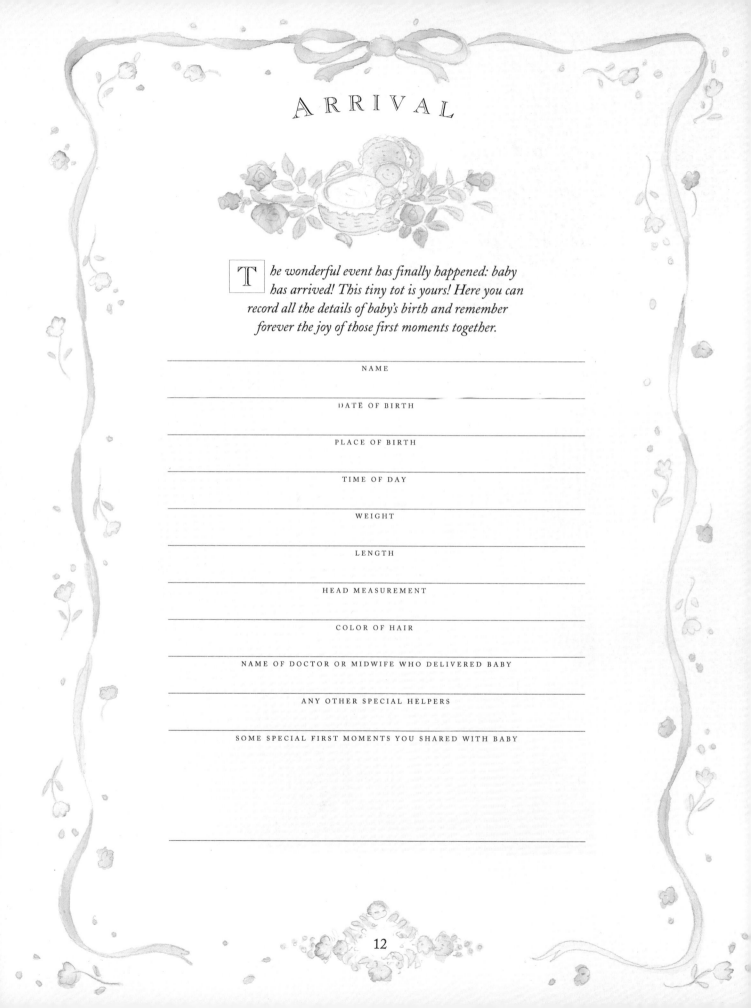

The wonderful event has finally happened: baby has arrived! This tiny tot is yours! Here you can record all the details of baby's birth and remember forever the joy of those first moments together.

_____
NAME

_____
DATE OF BIRTH

_____
PLACE OF BIRTH

_____
TIME OF DAY

_____
WEIGHT

_____
LENGTH

_____
HEAD MEASUREMENT

_____
COLOR OF HAIR

_____
NAME OF DOCTOR OR MIDWIFE WHO DELIVERED BABY

_____
ANY OTHER SPECIAL HELPERS

_____
SOME SPECIAL FIRST MOMENTS YOU SHARED WITH BABY

_____

ARRIVAL

FIRST
PHOTOGRAPHS

ARRIVAL

PHOTOGRAPHS
AND MEMORABILIA

Only a baby small,
Dropped from the skies;
Only a laughing face,
Two sunny eyes.

Only two cherry lips,
One chubby nose;
Only two little hands,
Ten little toes.

Only a golden head,
Curly and soft;
Only a tongue that wags
Loudly and oft.

Only a tender flower
Sent us to rear;
Only a life to love
While we are here.
MATTHIAS BARR

14

ARRIVAL

PHOTOGRAPHS
AND MEMORABILIA

H E L L O !

E ven in the first few days, it's funny how your tiny baby can bear an uncanny resemblance to someone else in the family – or not look like any of you at all! Who said what when they saw baby for the first time? Write down the funny and the thoughtful comments family and friends made.

PHOTOGRAPH   PHOTOGRAPH

_____
MOTHER'S FIRST WORDS AFTER BIRTH

_____
FATHER'S FIRST WORDS AFTER BIRTH

_____
FIRST IMPRESSIONS OF FAMILY AND FRIENDS

_____
WHO THOUGHT BABY LOOKED LIKE WHO

_____

H E L L O !

PHOTOGRAPHS
AND MEMENTOES

I am the family face;
Flesh perishes, I live on
Projecting trait and trace.
Through time to times anon,
And leaping from place to place.
Over oblivion.
THOMAS HARDY

CONGRATULATIONS

E veryone's overjoyed to hear baby has been born safely and they can't wait to come and see you both. It's a time for family and friends to make a well-deserved fuss of you. Here you can record everyone who came to visit or sent a card to wish you well.

FIRST VISITORS

FLOWERS FROM:

CARDS FROM:

GIFTS FROM:

CONGRATULATIONS

PHOTOGRAPHS

Life is a great bundle of little things.
OLIVER WENDELL HOLMES

19

A SPECIAL SOMEBODY

For your very special baby there will be some messages and cards you'll always want to remember. Here you can keep some of those special cards and little mementoes and any announcements that were made about baby's birth in the newspaper or elsewhere. Press a few little flowers too, from any special bouquets you were sent so that you never forget the kind wishes that were sent to you.

MEMENTOES

A SPECIAL SOMEBODY

FAVORITE CARDS
AND SPECIAL MESSAGES

The world has no such flowers in any land,
And no such pearl in any gulf of the sea,
As any babe on any mother's knee.
ALGERNON SWINBURNE

A SPECIAL DAY

T he day baby was born is certainly a very special day. Ask members of
the family to put down any special memories they have of that day and
what they were doing when they heard the good news that baby had arrived
safely. You could also note down any famous people or historical characters who
share your baby's special day.

_____

DAY OF THE WEEK ON WHICH BABY WAS BORN

_____

WHO SHARES BABY'S BIRTHDAY

_____

Monday's child is fair of face.
Tuesday's child is full of grace.
Wednesday's child is full of woe.
Thursday's child has far to go.
Friday's child is loving and giving.
Saturday's child works hard for its living:
And a child that is born on the Sabbath day,
Is fair, and wise, and good, and gay.
ANON

A SPECIAL DAY

WHAT FAMILY AND FRIENDS WERE DOING
WHEN BABY WAS BORN

A MARVELOUS MONTH

I t's also a marvelous month when baby arrives. Each one has a special stone and flower. Find out which is right for your precious little gem or beautiful blossom.

SPECIAL FLOWERS

JANUARY *Snowdrop*
A birth early in the year means baby is as pure as newly-fallen snow.

FEBRUARY *Carnation*
Bold and brave, baby shows great courage.

MARCH *Violet*
A blushing baby, filled with modesty and uncertain when undressed.

APRIL *Lily*
An infant that looks up to you with virtue in its eye.

MAY *Hawthorn*
This little blossom brims with brightness and new hope every day.

JUNE *Rose*
Simply a beautiful baby.

JULY *Daisy*
Wide-eyed and innocent.

AUGUST *Poppy*
An infant that fills the world with color but has a pleasantly peaceful nature.

SEPTEMBER *Morning Glory*
This little glory is easily contented.

OCTOBER *Cosmos*
Crawling out of the cot with early ambition.

NOVEMBER *Chrysanthemum*
A cheeky, cheerful sunny child.

DECEMBER *Holly*
Baby's good at working out what's round the corner.

A MARVELLOUS MONTH

B aby's bound to be a little gem.
Which special stone belongs to
your little one?

SPECIAL STONES

JANUARY *Garnet*
Baby has a steady, constant nature.

FEBRUARY *Amethyst*
Sincerity will show as baby grows.

MARCH *Bloodstone*
Baby's building up lots of courage for future use.

APRIL *Diamond*
A real gem, who dazzles you with those innocent eyes.

MAY *Emerald*
Baby brings sheer happiness.

JUNE *Pearl*
A precious, pristine infant.

JULY *Ruby*
Baby's born for better things and may behave majestically.

AUGUST *Moonstone*
Great joy surrounds this child.

SEPTEMBER *Sapphire*
A bright baby who shines at everything.

OCTOBER *Opal*
This tiny tot is filled with future hopes.

NOVEMBER *Topaz*
The most loyal and devoted of infants.

DECEMBER *Turquoise*
Without a doubt, success and seeing ahead are given to this baby.

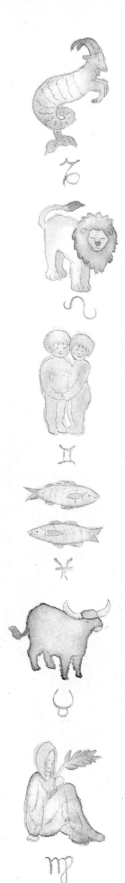

W hat do the stars have in store for your baby? It all depends on the sign of the Zodiac your baby was born under, the sign through which the sun is passing at the time of the birth. For astrologers to make a closer study of baby's character and future, they will need to find out the exact position of the moon and planets as well as the sun at your baby's birth. They can work this out if they have the time, date and place of birth.

PHOTOGRAPH

EXACT TIME OF BIRTH

DATE

PLACE

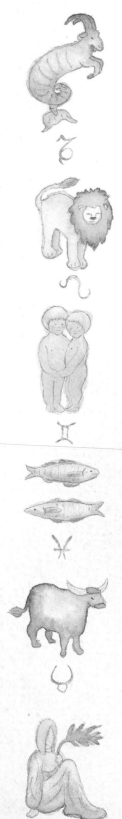

BABY'S BIRTHSIGN

ARIES *March 21-April 20*
Bold, brave, confident and full of energy; very mobile and an early walker.

TAURUS *April 21-May 21*
Good natured, contented and determined, with smiles for everyone; loves food.

GEMINI *May 22-June 21*
Lively, playful, vivacious, friendly and inquisitive; an early talker.

CANCER *June 22-July 22*
Shy, sensitive and affectionate; likes lots of cuddles and teddies to look after.

LEO *July 23-August 23*
Sunny, strong, happy and exuberant, a little prince or princess; adores an audience.

VIRGO *August 24-September 23*
Neat, quiet and solemn; very clever with hands and starts building very early.

LIBRA *September 24-October 23*
Romantic charmer and outrageous flirt; will twist everyone round a chubby little finger in no time.

SCORPIO *October 24-November 22*
Pensive and imaginative, with a store of hidden energy; needs lots of security and thrives on routine.

SAGITTARIUS *November 23-December 21*
Cheerful, chatty, extrovert and adventurous; the first out of the playpen.

CAPRICORN *December 22-January 20*
Self-possessed and intelligent with unique sense of humor, usually musical and an early reader.

AQUARIUS *January 21-February 19*
Bright, independent of mind and unpredictable; an unconventional babe with a will of iron.

PISCES *February 20-March 20*
Dreamy, imaginative and intuitive, with rainbow moods of tears and smiles; loves water play.

READ ALL ABOUT IT!

T he world's a very big place to be born into.
What was happening at the time of baby's birth?
Cut out some newspaper pictures and stories that record the crises
and funny things that happened that day in the big wide world.

PHOTOGRAPH

WORLD EVENTS

FAMOUS WORLD LEADERS

LOCAL NEWS

READ ALL ABOUT IT!

HEADLINES AND
BIRTHDAY SCOOPS

The world is so full of a number of things,
I'm sure we should all be as happy as kings.
ROBERT LOUIS STEVENSON

29

SIGNS OF THE TIMES

F ashions come and fashions go and there's nothing funnier than
looking back and remembering what was in vogue a few years ago.
Write down some favorites at the time that baby was born and you
can all look back and laugh in the future!

_____
POPULAR ATHLETES
_____
POPULAR ACTORS AND ACTRESSES
_____
POPULAR COMEDIANS
_____
POPULAR SINGERS
_____
POPULAR MUSICIANS AND BANDS
_____
FILM OF THE YEAR
_____
BOOK OF THE YEAR
_____
POPULAR TV PROGRAMS
_____
WHAT WE WERE WEARING
_____
POPULAR CARS
_____
FADS OF THE YEAR
_____
HOW MUCH?

A pint of milk: A loaf of bread: A bar of chocolate:
_____

CUTTINGS AND EPHEMERA

Men are more like the times they live in than they are like their fathers.
ALI IBN-ABI-TALIB

WELCOME HOME

T here's no place like home! It's a great relief to get baby home, if born in a hospital or elsewhere. It takes time to settle the newcomer in but they'll soon start to sense they've arrived at the safest, happiest place in the world – your home.

WHEN YOU CAME HOME (if born in a hospital)

_____

DAY AND DATE

_____

TIME

_____

WEATHER

_____

PHOTOGRAPH

WELCOME HOME

PHOTOGRAPH

WHO BROUGHT BABY HOME

WHAT BABY WORE

WHO WAS ALREADY WAITING AT HOME

O fortunate, O happy day,
When a new household finds its place
Among the myriad homes of earth,
Like a new star just sprung to birth.
HENRY WADSWORTH LONGFELLOW

33

WELCOME HOME

HOW BABY SETTLED IN

WHAT BABY'S ROOM IS LIKE

BABY'S ROOM

WELCOME HOME

PHOTOGRAPH   PHOTOGRAPH

PHOTOGRAPH

Home is where the great are small, and the small are great.
ANON

OUR FAMILY

H ere's a place to put in photographs
of all the family, to introduce baby
to all your relatives.

PHOTOGRAPH

_____   _____
MOTHER   FATHER

_____   _____
NAME   NAME

_____   _____
WHERE BORN   WHERE BORN

_____   _____
BIRTHDAY   BIRTHDAY

_____   _____

OUR FAMILY

MOTHER'S MOTHER	MOTHER'S FATHER
WHERE BORN	WHERE BORN
BIRTHDAY	BIRTHDAY

PHOTOGRAPHS

FATHER'S MOTHER	FATHER'S FATHER
WHERE BORN	WHERE BORN
BIRTHDAY	BIRTHDAY

37

BEFORE YOU WERE BORN

If mother and father had never met, well, baby wouldn't even exist, so everyone's very glad they got together!

PHOTOGRAPH

WHAT WORK THEY DID

MOTHER   FATHER

SPECIAL INTERESTS AND HOBBIES

MOTHER   FATHER

WHEN THEY MET

WHERE THEY MET

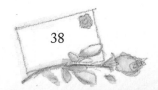

BEFORE YOU WERE BORN

PHOTOGRAPHS AND MEMENTOES

We never know the love of our parents for us
till we have become parents.
HENRY WARD BEECHER

39

OUR FAMILY TREE

GREAT GREAT GRANDMOTHER

GREAT GREAT GRANDFATHER

GREAT GRANDMOTHER

GREAT GRANDFATHER

GRANDMOTHER

GRANDFATHER

AUNTS & UNCLES

MOTHER

SISTER

SISTER

BABY

OUR FAMILY TREE

GREAT GREAT GRANDFATHER

GREAT GREAT GRANDMOTHER

GREAT GRANDMOTHER

GREAT GRANDFATHER

GRANDFATHER

GRANDMOTHER

FATHER

AUNTS & UNCLES

BROTHER

BROTHER

41

FAMILY AND FRIENDS

I t's wonderful for baby to find there's a whole load of family and friends beyond the ones already met. Here's a place to put some pictures of baby's expanding family and write down who everyone is, too.

A faithful friend is the medicine of life.
ECCLESIASTES

42

FAMILY AND FRIENDS

_____

BABY'S BROTHERS AND SISTERS

_____

BABY'S AUNTS AND UNCLES

_____

BABY'S COUSINS

_____

FAVORITE FAMILY FRIENDS

_____

PHOTOGRAPH

Whenever Auntie moves around,
Her dresses make a curious sound;
They trail behind her up the floor,
And trundle after through the door.
ROBERT LOUIS STEVENSON

43

FUN FIRSTS

There's nothing quite as exciting as watching your baby discovering some wonderful new things about the world. Here are some special firsts to keep on record:

FIRST SMILES

FIRST LAUGHS ALOUD

FIRST DISCOVERS HANDS

FIRST DISCOVERS FEET

STARTS TO GRASP OBJECTS

FIRST NOTICES A MOBILE

EYES ABLE TO FOLLOW A MOVING OBJECT

TURNS HEAD TO FOLLOW AN OBJECT

RECOGNIZES MOTHER

RECOGNIZES FATHER

FUN FIRSTS

STARTS TO HOLD UP HEAD

ROLLS HEAD FROM SIDE TO BACK

KICKS AND WAVES ARMS AND LIES FLAT ON BACK

DOES TINY 'PRESS-UPS' LYING ON TUMMY

ROLLS FROM TUMMY TO BACK

PHOTOGRAPH

*'When the first baby laughed for the first time, the laugh broke into a
thousand pieces and they all went skipping about, and that was the beginning of fairies.'*
SIR J M BARRIE

BABY'S GETTING BIGGER

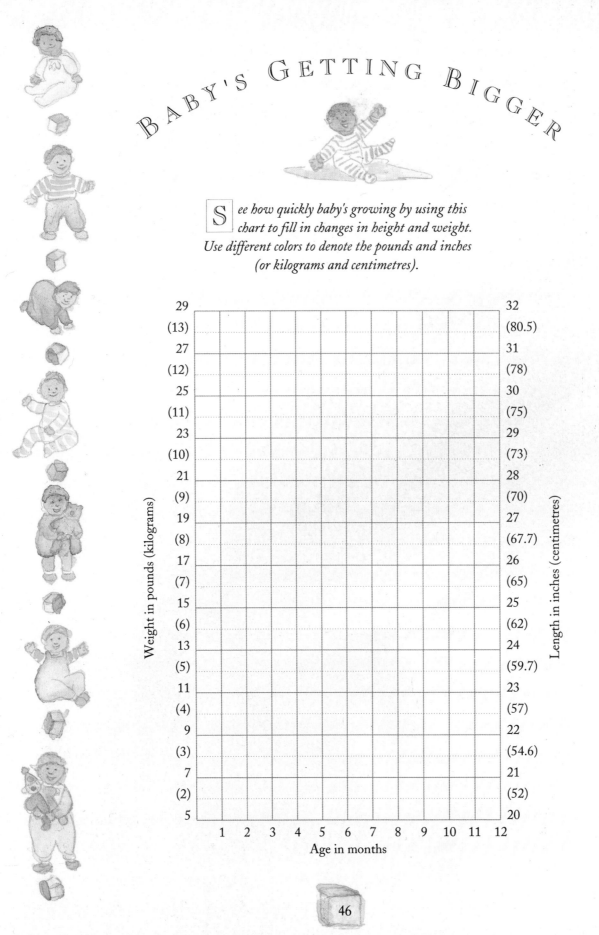

S ee how quickly baby's growing by using this
chart to fill in changes in height and weight.
*Use different colors to denote the pounds and inches
(or kilograms and centimetres).*

Weight in pounds (kilograms)

	29												32	
(13)													(80.5)	
	27												31	
(12)													(78)	

Age in months

Length in inches (centimetres)

46

BABY'S GETTING BIGGER

TINY TRACES

Here's another way to see how baby's growing. Trace round baby's tiny hands and feet. See the difference between six weeks, six months and one year.

He is so small, he does not know
The summer sun, the winter snow;
The spring that ebbs and comes again,
All this is far beyond his ken.

A little world he feels and sees:
His mother's arms, his mother's knees;
He hides his face against her breast,
And does not care to learn the rest.
CHRISTOPHER MORLEY

FROM SITTING TO STANDING

*I*t's both funny and touching to see baby struggling to stand. First there's the crawl to conquer, then there's little exercises to stretch those little legs. Finally, baby finds its feet and starts to wobble round the room. Then one day, you'll see baby walk without any help and suddenly your little baby has turned into a toddler.

BABY SITS SUPPORTED

BABY SITS FOR A FEW SECONDS UNSUPPORTED

BABY TRIES TO CRAWL

BABY CAN CRAWL

BABY STANDS WHEN HELD

BABY STANDS JUST HOLDING YOUR HANDS

BABY CAN PULL SELF UP TO STAND

BABY WOBBLES ROUND CLUTCHING FURNITURE

BABY WALKS WITH SUPPORT

BABY CLIMBS THE STAIRS

BABY WALKS WITHOUT HELP

48

FROM SITTING TO STANDING

PHOTOGRAPHS

A journey of a thousand miles must with a single step begin.
CHINESE PROVERB

49

Time To Talk

Baby will try to talk to you from Day One. It may just be a gurgle or a 'ga-ga' but it's not easy being a baby and trying to talk. Soon you'll learn to understand what's being said, then one day, baby will start to speak a language everyone can understand

_____

FIRST GURGLE

_____

FIRST 'GAA' OR OTHER SOUNDS

_____

FIRST SOUNDS SUGGESTING ENJOYMENT

_____

FIRST SEEMS TO RECOGNIZE ITS NAME

_____

FIRST SHOUTS FOR ATTENTION

_____

PHOTOGRAPH

TIME TO TALK

A word is dead
When it is said,
Some say.
I say it just
Begins to live
That day.
EMILY DICKINSON

PHOTOGRAPH

FIRST REAL WORD

FIRST MADE-UP WORDS AND MEANING

BABY'S SPECIAL WORDS FOR

Toys   Family   Friends   Other Objects

THE SOUND OF SILENCE

S leep is vital for both mother and baby.
It takes time for baby to find a pattern
but once a routine is established, everyone will
start to sleep more easily.

BABY'S FAVORITE SLEEPING POSITION

CRIB
OR CRADLE

BABY'S SLEEPING PATTERN AT:

1 Month	3 Months	6 Months
12 Months	18 Months	24 Months

FIRST NIGHT BABY SLEPT RIGHT THROUGH THE NIGHT

FAVORITE COMFORTS

FAVORITE BEDTIME TOYS

FAVORITE THINGS THAT HELP BABY NOD OFF

Niddedy, noddledy, to and fro,
Tired and sleepy, to bed we go.
Jump into bed,
Blow out the light,
Head on the pillow,
Shut your eyes tight.
ANON

THE SOUND OF SILENCE

PHOTOGRAPHS

HAPPY AND HEALTHY

I t's worth making a note of all the trials
and tribulations of childhood illnesses, shots
and any allergies. It's a handy reminder of when
shots are due and any other information you might need.

FIRST VISIT TO CLINIC OR DOCTOR

NAME OF BABY'S DOCTOR

NOTES

*Early to bed
And early to rise,
Is the way to be healthy
And wealthy and wise.*
ANON

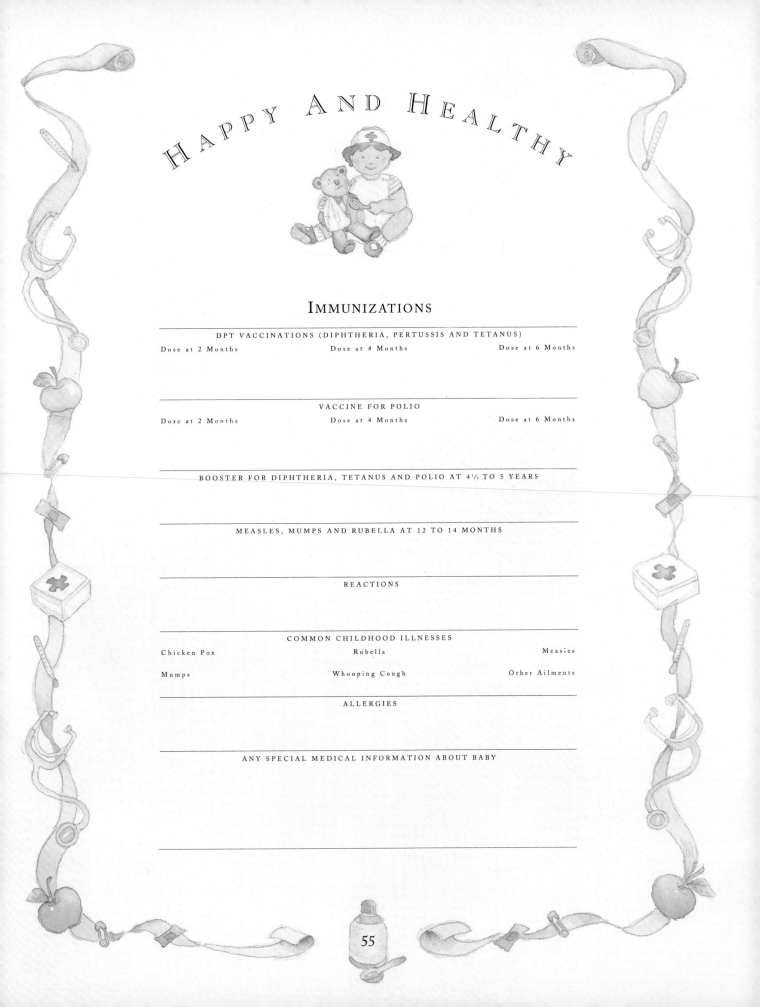

H A P P Y A N D H E A L T H Y

IMMUNIZATIONS

DPT VACCINATIONS (DIPHTHERIA, PERTUSSIS AND TETANUS)

Dose at 2 Months   Dose at 4 Months   Dose at 6 Months

VACCINE FOR POLIO

Dose at 2 Months   Dose at 4 Months   Dose at 6 Months

BOOSTER FOR DIPHTHERIA, TETANUS AND POLIO AT 4½ TO 5 YEARS

MEASLES, MUMPS AND RUBELLA AT 12 TO 14 MONTHS

REACTIONS

COMMON CHILDHOOD ILLNESSES

Chicken Pox   Rubella   Measles

Mumps   Whooping Cough   Other Ailments

ALLERGIES

ANY SPECIAL MEDICAL INFORMATION ABOUT BABY

TINY TEETH

T he agony and ecstasy of teething are all part of growing. First teeth are a great triumph for baby and must feel very funny. Use these pages to note down the arrival of milk teeth and add photographs charting gummy grins to toothy smiles.

DATE FIRST TOOTH APPEARED

FIRST CHEWED A TEETHING RING

FIRST TIME TEETH WERE BRUSHED

FIRST TIME BABY BRUSHED OWN TEETH

Through the house what busy joy,
Just because the infant boy
Has a tiny tooth to show!
I have got a double row,
All as white, and all as small;
Yet no one cares for mine at all.
CHARLES AND MARY LAMB

TINY TEETH

PHOTOGRAPHS

57

ENJOYING EATING

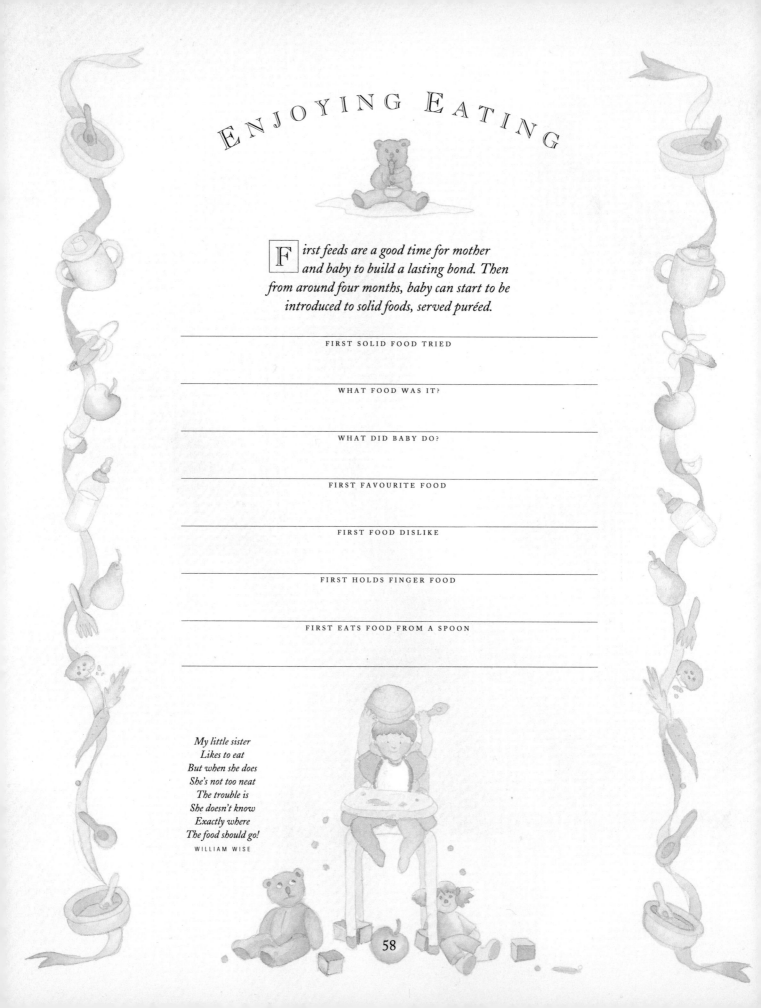

First feeds are a good time for mother and baby to build a lasting bond. Then from around four months, baby can start to be introduced to solid foods, served puréed.

FIRST SOLID FOOD TRIED

WHAT FOOD WAS IT?

WHAT DID BABY DO?

FIRST FAVOURITE FOOD

FIRST FOOD DISLIKE

FIRST HOLDS FINGER FOOD

FIRST EATS FOOD FROM A SPOON

My little sister
Likes to eat
But when she does
She's not too neat
The trouble is
She doesn't know
Exactly where
The food should go!
WILLIAM WISE

ENJOYING EATING

PHOTOGRAPH

FIRST HOLDS THE SPOON

FIRST DRINK FROM A CUP WITH A SPOUT

FIRST DRINK FROM AN ORDINARY CUP

FIRST FAVOURITE DRINK

FUNNY EATING HABITS

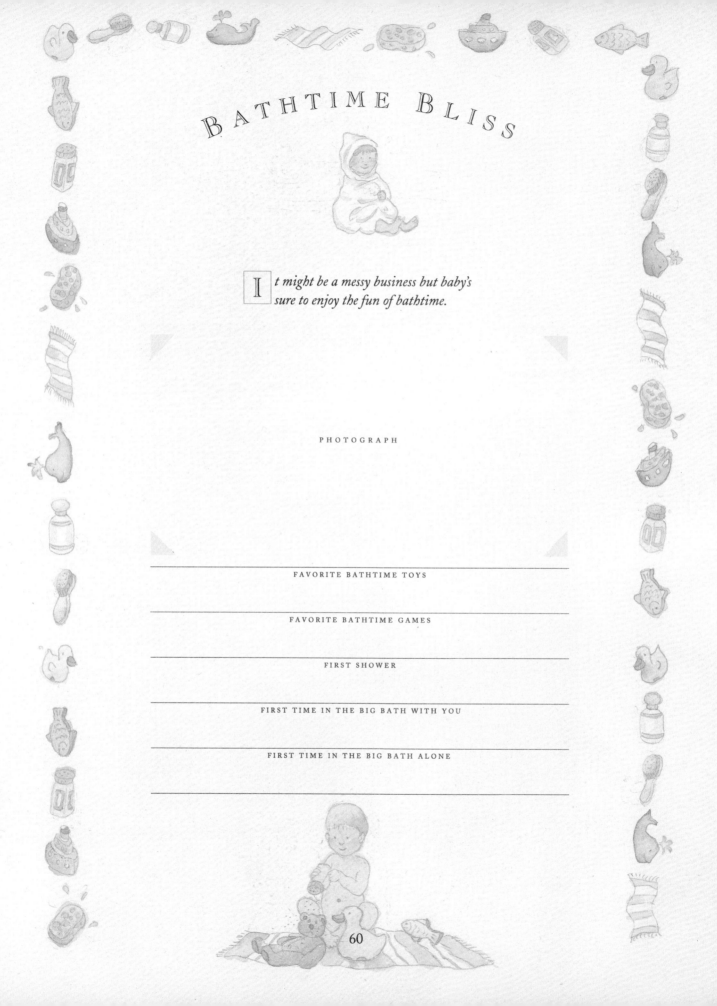

BATHTIME BLISS

I *t might be a messy business but baby's sure to enjoy the fun of bathtime.*

PHOTOGRAPH

FAVORITE BATHTIME TOYS

FAVORITE BATHTIME GAMES

FIRST SHOWER

FIRST TIME IN THE BIG BATH WITH YOU

FIRST TIME IN THE BIG BATH ALONE

60

BATHTIME BLISS

PHOTOGRAPHS

Rub-a-dub-dub
Three men in a tub,
And how do you think they got there?
The butcher, the baker,
The candlestick-maker.
They all jumped out of a rotten potato
'Twas enough to make a man stare.

ANON

61

PLAYTIME

Y ou get to know baby better and
baby gets to know you too, as
you play together. All the time, baby is
learning new skills in the simplest ways.

FIRSTS PLAYS 'PAT-A-CAKE'

FIRST PLAYS 'PEEK-A-BOO'

FIRST PUTS BUILDING BRICKS ON TOP OF EACH OTHER

GAMES YOU PLAY TOGETHER

TOYS YOU PLAY WITH

STORIES YOU SHARE

NAMES OF BABY'S PLAYMATES

Pat-a-cake, pat-a-cake, baker's man.
Bake me a cake as fast as you can;
Pat it and prick it and mark it with B,
Put it in the oven for baby and me.
ANON

62

PLAYTIME

PHOTOGRAPH   PHOTOGRAPH

PHOTOGRAPH

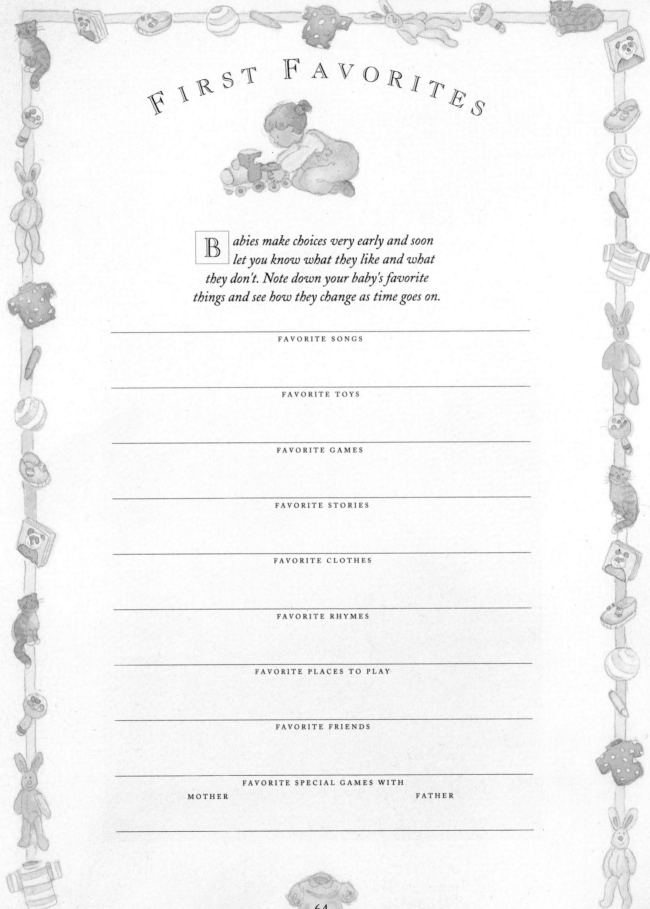

FIRST FAVORITES

abies make choices very early and soon let you know what they like and what they don't. Note down your baby's favorite things and see how they change as time goes on.

_____

FAVORITE SONGS

_____

FAVORITE TOYS

_____

FAVORITE GAMES

_____

FAVORITE STORIES

_____

FAVORITE CLOTHES

_____

FAVORITE RHYMES

_____

FAVORITE PLACES TO PLAY

_____

FAVORITE FRIENDS

_____

FAVORITE SPECIAL GAMES WITH

MOTHER   FATHER

_____

FIRST FAVORITES

PHOTOGRAPHS

When I am grown to man's estate
I shall be very proud and great,
And tell the other girls and boys
Not to meddle with my toys.
ROBERT LOUIS STEVENSON

EARLY TRIPS OUTSIDE

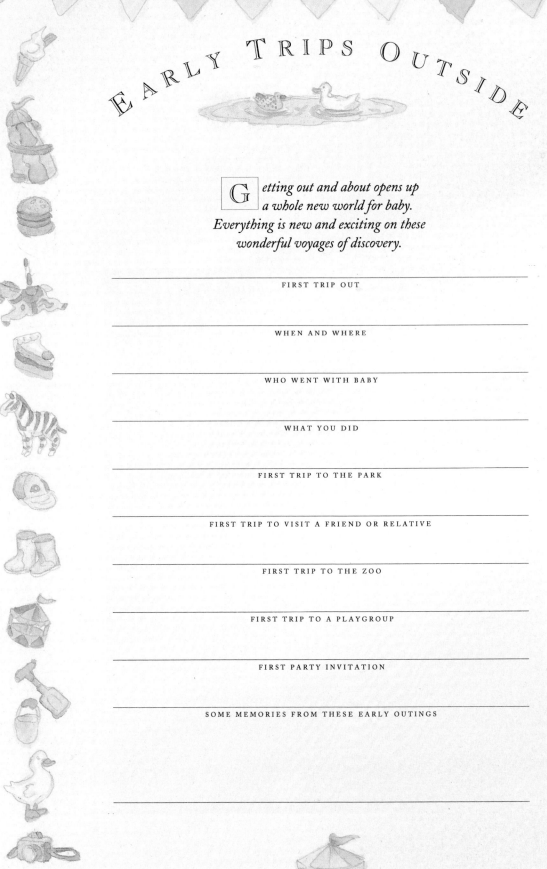

G etting out and about opens up
a whole new world for baby.
Everything is new and exciting on these
wonderful voyages of discovery.

FIRST TRIP OUT

WHEN AND WHERE

WHO WENT WITH BABY

WHAT YOU DID

FIRST TRIP TO THE PARK

FIRST TRIP TO VISIT A FRIEND OR RELATIVE

FIRST TRIP TO THE ZOO

FIRST TRIP TO A PLAYGROUP

FIRST PARTY INVITATION

SOME MEMORIES FROM THESE EARLY OUTINGS

EARLY TRIPS OUTSIDE

PHOTOGRAPHS

First I saw the white bear, then I saw the black;
Then I saw the camel with a hump upon his back;
Then I saw the grey wolf, with mutton in his maw;
Then I saw the wombat waddle in the straw;
Then I saw the elephant a-waving of his trunk;
Then I saw the monkeys – mercy, how unpleasantly they – smelt!

WILLIAM MAKEPEACE THACKERAY

EARLY TRIPS OUTSIDE

GETTING ABOUT

FIRST RIDE IN A STROLLER/CARRIAGE

FIRST TRIP IN A CAR

FIRST TRIP ON A TRAIN

FIRST TRIP ON A PLANE

FIRST TRIP ON A BOAT

PHOTOGRAPH

EARLY TRIPS OUTSIDE

PHOTOGRAPH   PHOTOGRAPH

PHOTOGRAPH

Three plum buns
To eat here at the stile
In the clover meadow,
For we have walked a mile.

One for you, and one for me,
And one left over:
Give it to the boy who shouts
To scare sheep from the clover.
CHRISTINA ROSSETTI

HAPPY BIRTHDAY

B aby's first birthday is a super celebration of a wonderful year. Although baby might wonder what the fuss is about, it's fun to have a party anyway. Keep any special cards and mementoes from the party and stick them down here.

PHOTOGRAPH

_____

BABY'S FIRST BIRTHDAY PRESENTS

_____

WHO GAVE THEM TO BABY

_____

TIME AND PLACE OF BIRTHDAY PARTY

_____

PARTY GUESTS

_____

Happy Birthday

FIRST BIRTHDAY CARDS
MEMENTOES FROM THE PARTY

H A P P Y   B I R T H D A Y

PHOTOGRAPH   PHOTOGRAPH

PHOTOGRAPH

HAPPY BIRTHDAY

MEMENTOES

Grandma's baked a cake for me.
See the candles, one, two, three.
Put them out with one big blow.
Ready, steady, here we go.
ANON

FESTIVE FUN

[T] here's nothing like sharing seasonal celebrations with a little one. Whether it's Christmas or another festive occasion on your calendar, baby will want to join in all the fun.

PHOTOGRAPH

_____
BABY'S FIRST FESTIVE OCCASION

_____
WHERE IT WAS SPENT

_____
WHO WAS THERE

_____
PRESENTS THE FAMILY GAVE TO BABY

_____
PRESENTS AND CARDS FROM FRIENDS

_____
FUNNY FESTIVE MOMENTS WITH BABY
_____

FESTIVE FUN

PHOTOGRAPHS
CARDS
FESTIVE MEMENTOES

I love to go to parties
And spoil all the fun
By sitting in the custard tarts
And throwing buttered buns.
JOHN JENKIN

OUR SPECIAL STAR

Baby is your very special star. As infants grow, they love to try to catch your attention with their antics, acting the fool or dressing up in disguise. Music is also one of baby's first and favorite ways to show off special talent – or just make a very loud noise.

FIRST CLAPS HANDS

MOVES IN RHYTHM TO MUSIC

MAKES BANGING NOISES

FIRST FAVORITE SONG

FIRST DRESSES UP

FIRST DOES A DANCE

FIRST PERFORMS A PARTY PIECE

OTHER EARLY SIGNS OF STARDOM

OUR SPECIAL STAR

PHOTOGRAPH OF THE STAR

*Something you consider bad may bring out your child's talents;
something you consider good may stifle them.*
CHÂTEAUBRIAND

HAPPY VACATIONS

F irst vacations together with baby are bound to be fun. Write down some of the best moments, so that you can recall them again in the future.

PHOTOGRAPH

PHOTOGRAPH

Happy Vacations

VACATION SNAPS

When I was down beside the sea
A wooden spade they gave to me
To dig the sandy shore.
My holes were empty like a cup.
In every hole the sea came up
Till it could come no more.
ROBERT LOUIS STEVENSON.

HAPPY VACATIONS

PHOTOGRAPH

FIRST TRIP TO THE BEACH

PLACE

FIRST SWIM

THINGS YOU DID TOGETHER

HAPPY VACATIONS

VACATION SNAPS
AND HAPPY MEMORIES

IN THE PICTURE

O nce they have worked out one end of the crayon from the other, all infants love to show off their artistic abilities. You'll want to treasure these drawings forever, so keep them safely stuck on these pages.

FIRST PICTURES

_____

BABY FIRST HOLDS A CRAYON

_____

DATE OF FIRST PICTURE

_____

IN THE PICTURE

FIRST PICTURES

In later years they're bound to say
Our loved one showed talent from an early day.
ANON

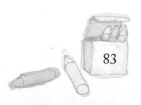

TRIALS AND TRIBULATIONS

O nce baby starts to move about, so will everything else. All sorts of precious objects will get broken, you'll find the cat in the playpen, a saucepan stuck on baby's head and grandpa's false teeth hidden behind the sofa. Write down some of the silly mishaps and naughty moments your little devil has got up to.

PHOTOGRAPH

We are dismayed when we find
that even disaster cannot cure us of our faults.
VAUVENARGUES

TRIALS AND TRIBULATIONS

PHOTOGRAPH

PHOTOGRAPH

PHOTOGRAPH

BRAVE AND BONNY

There's nothing quite as sweet as the occasional innocent caring and sharing of an infant. Write down some of the little incidents and touching moments which have almost brought you to tears. Perhaps your child has shown a little kindness to a tiny friend or overwhelmed you with a sudden burst of affection.

PHOTOGRAPH

By chivalries as tiny,
A blossom, or a book,
The seeds of smiles are planted –
Which blossom in the dark.
EMILY DICKINSON

86

BRAVE AND BONNY

PHOTOGRAPH

PHOTOGRAPH

SPECIAL CEREMONIES

Y ou may be bringing baby up
within a religion. Here you can
write about any special ceremonies which
baby has attended or been involved in.

_____

TYPE OF CEREMONY (e.g. Christening)

_____

DATE

_____

PLACE

_____

WHO WAS THERE

_____

GIFTS RECEIVED

_____

BABY'S FULL NAME

_____

THE MEANING OF BABY'S NAMES

_____

WHY THE NAMES WERE CHOSEN

_____

WHO CHOSE THEM

_____

SPECIAL CEREMONIES

PHOTOGRAPH

For a very special day
Dress up baby bonny and gay
Happy, playful, clean and chubby
By day's end, he'll be looking grubby.
LAVINIA LEE

THOUGHTS FOR THE FUTURE

*W*hat will baby become? Everyone likes to guess at what baby will grow up to be. Maybe you see early signs now – if baby's always driving a toy car, will this little infant become a race car driver? Here's a place to write down what family and friends think your baby will do in the future. When baby's old enough, write down what baby says it wants for the future, too.

WHAT YOU THINK WILL BECOME OF BABY

WHAT FRIENDS AND FAMILY PREDICTS

WHAT YOUR BABY HOPES WILL HAPPEN

PHOTOGRAPH

I often wish I were a king,
And then I could do anything.
WALTER DE LA MARE

THOUGHTS FOR THE FUTURE

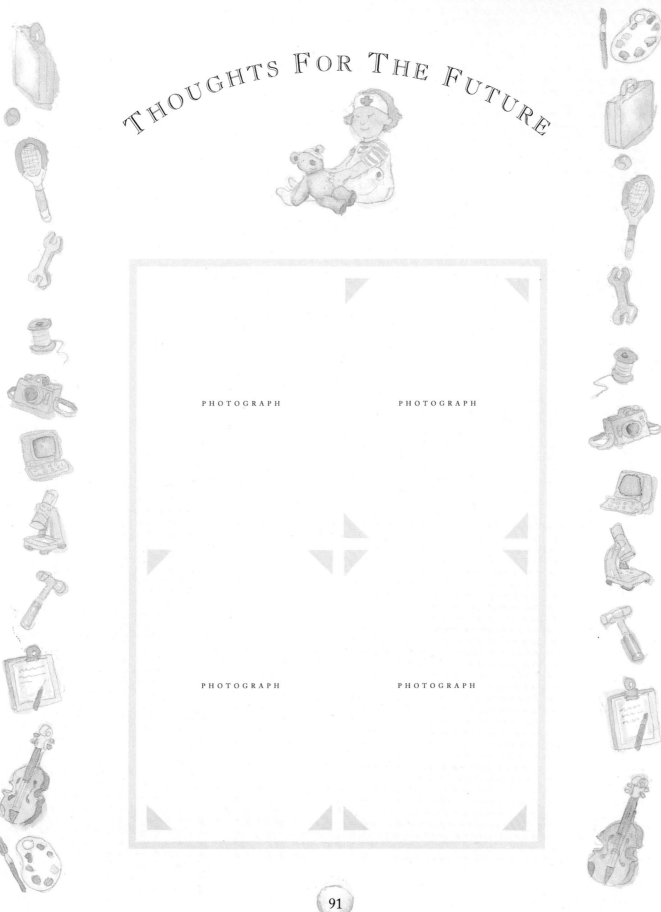

PHOTOGRAPH

PHOTOGRAPH

PHOTOGRAPH

PHOTOGRAPH

WITH LOTS OF LOVE

This is a very special page for you to invite family and friends to write in wishes and other messages for your child's future. In later life, your child might like to read the hopes and aspirations you had for the times ahead. For family and friends who are not around to write in this book, stick in any special messages they send, with lots of love, to your baby.

_____

_____

_____

_____

_____

_____

_____

_____

You may give your children your love but not your thoughts,
For they have their own thoughts.
You may house their bodies but not their souls,
For their souls dwell in the house of tomorrow, which you cannot
visit, not even in your dreams.
KAHLIL GIBRAN

92